The Gods
in a time of Corona

Bernie Neville

First published 2020
by Carlavanlaar.com
27 Wilson Avenue, Brunswick, Victoria 3056, Australia.

ISBN 978-0-6487679-4-7

The Gods
in a time of Corona

The glorious gifts of the gods are not to be cast aside.

Homer

The use of the Greco-Roman gods as metaphors for different per-spectives on life, different patterns of behaviour, different constella-tions of values, needs, instincts and habits, has been conventional in most of European history. When Jung developed his archetypal the-ory, he continued in this poetic tradition, finding the manifestations of the gods in personal and collective behaviour and convinced that the archetypal images are most powerfully and resonantly manifested in the great myths. Contemporary archetypal psychologists contin-ue to use the same language and share the same conviction. They concentrate their attention on the patterns they find in our ways of apprehending the universe and of acting in it. They are fascinated by the recurring patterns in our ways of imagining the world, in our cul-tural movements, in our architecture, in our scientific paradigms, in our dreams, in our diseases, in our obsessions, in our relationships, in our organizations, in our yearnings, in our political ideologies. They find that mythical or metaphorical thinking offers a fruitful way of exploring them.

Each of the god-images personifies a 'mode of apprehension' (Jung's term) which gives a distinct and observable shape to our encounter with the world. In the current global emergency, each god-image gives a distinct and observable shape to our understanding of our problems and their resolution.

The key energies which move us in our encounter with the world are those which the classical Greeks identified as gods. There are plenty of people who are taken over by an obsession with wealth, pleasure or technology (or love, curiosity or alcohol) so that they appear to be no longer in control of their actions. The ancient Greeks and other polytheistic peoples would see here the presence and action of a god who has a name, a personality and a story. We may pride ourselves on our rationality, on our detachment from such superstitions, but there are levels of our consciousness at which we still respond to the world and its events in the magical-mythical ways of our biological and cultural ancestors. And there are times when we are overpowered, individually or collectively, by a force - desire, rage, panic, depression - which pre-scientific cultures would have recognized as a god. Jung used the word 'inflation' to depict the condition in which an individual is taken over by an archetypal energy. When someone fell into a rage in Ancient Greece, friends and enemies could see that the god of war, Ares, had temporarily taken possession. Likewise, if someone fell in love, it was clear that Eros had taken control. A woman obsessed with mothering her newborn was clearly possessed by Demeter. If someone was in deep depression Hades, the god of the Underworld, was clearly at work. A crowd gripped by panic must have been taken over by Pan.

We can also talk of cultural inflation, where a nation or culture has become totally dominated by a particular archetypal energy. Jung saw Hitler's Germany to be inflated by Dionysus. We are all too familiar with the energy of Ares overcoming rational thinking and pushing a nation into war. The Global Financial Crisis of a decade ago can readily be seen as an inflation of the global financial system by Hermes, the unpredictable and deceiving god of the market place.[1]

The cultural inflation we associate with Hermes has been dominant in Australia for four decades and Hermes is prominent in the current rhetoric concerning COVID19 and our ways of dealing with it.

When we hear from our Prime Minister that the secret of economic recovery in Australia is greater deregulation, it is Hermes speaking.

The myths of the classical Greeks are not the stories of a stone age tribe, though they may have begun as such. They are the myths of an urban, sophisticated, self-reflective people, with a complex social and political system, and a highly developed cultural life. The Greeks understood that there are forces in the cosmos which are bigger that any individual human, not just mechanical forces but forces like power, love, fear and rage, forces which have an existence beyond their manifestations in particular individual, forces which they personified and gave considerable respect. They wove a web of myths from many sources to represent the complexity of life, a web of overlapping and interpenetrating stories which provided a rich source of meaning for the philosophers and poets of the European Renaissance and which now serves the same function for contemporary archetypal psychologists. We should not dismiss myths, whatever their cultural context, as the products of a superstitious, unsophisticated people and of little relevance to us. Neither should we accept them as the ancient expressions of a universal immutable wisdom. Myths are an imaginative expression of a people's experience of what kind of universe they are living in. They articulate their experience of what Joseph Campbell calls 'the becoming thing that is not a thing at all but life, not as it will be or as it should be, as it *was* or as it never will be, but as it is, in *depth*, in *process, here and now, inside and out'.*[2]

The patterns we find in our lives in the twenty-first century are not new patterns. The stories through which we construct and express the meaning of our lives are not new stories. The conflicts between competing meanings and competing values are not new conflicts. The same squabbling gods whom Homer described are still present in our personalities, our technologies and our institutions. They squabble within us when we reflect on our current planetary emergencies. And they squabble within the arguments of our current decision makers as they try to determine an appropriate reaction to a catastrophic health crisis.

Jung understood the gods and the myths surrounding them to be manifestations of archetypal patterns. He had several ways of explaining what he meant by archetype, and his different explanations seem sometimes contradictory. If we follow Jung, archetypes sometimes appear to be metaphysical entities, independent of human experience. Sometimes they appear to be biological structures, hard-wired in our genes and in our brains and manifested in instinctual behaviour. Sometimes they appear to be abstract mental structures which shape our experience, without being experienced themselves. Jung does not seem to have cared much about being logically consistent, and was content with his observation that philosophy, biology, psychology, anthropology and religious studies all pointed in the same direction - towards the notion that our behaviour is shaped by innate mental structures which 'can only be explained by assuming them to be deposits of the constantly repeated experiences of humanity'[3]

Since Jung's time, the word archetype has been used in so many different and inconsistent ways that we could argue that it is useless as a scientific term. Nevertheless, we do recognize patterns in individual and group behaviour, patterns which appear to be universal across cultures. We recognize that many of the patterns that we observe today are the same as those are recorded in ancient mythologies and associated with the personalities of the gods. We recognize a pattern we call 'mothering', a pattern we call 'falling in love', a pattern we call 'getting even' and so on. And we now find that the sciences of brain and behaviour seem to point to something which, for want of a better word, we can continue to call archetype.

Pre-scientific societies have largely been convinced that everything has already happened in the time of the gods and that we merely act out their stories. Jung acknowledged the influence of Plato's theory of universal, transcendent forms on his ideas. In the twentieth century Jung's thinking on archetypes was paralleled by the work of structuralist philosophers like Levy- Strauss who pointed to the deep structures which shape our thinking and behaviour. We may think of ourselves as individuals, doing our own thinking, but we live in a universe of intersecting myths, of which we may be totally unaware. We may think of myths as stories which we have, but in reality, they have us.[4]

Cognitive scientists and evolutionary psychologists are not inclined to use the word 'archetype', however, even when they are arguing that we are born with innate instinctual knowledge inherited from our ancestors (for example, the instinctual tendency to use language, avoid danger and protect our children)[5]. Others argue that our genes do not carry any sort of blueprint for our behaviour. They argue that, rather than carrying information, our genes carry a tendency to focus on particular patterns in our environment (for example the human face) and interact with them. They suggest that we gradually construct a meaningful world through interacting with particular aspects of our environment. Our earliest experience is especially important. One of our first experiences - even before birth - is *containment,* from which we develop a sense of *inside* and *outside*. Other early experiences that we seem to be pre-disposed to notice are *path* (the sense of movement in a particular direction), *up-down, force, part-whole* and *link*. These *image schemas* can be thought of as our first step towards the appreciation of a meaningful universe.[6]

For anyone who is comfortable with the Jungian language of archetype this simply demonstrates what Jung intuited a long time ago. It made little difference to him whether we think there is a metaphysical entity which has a transcendent existence and manifests itself in our human experience of *containment* - a mother's womb, a mother's arms, a cave, a home, a family, a nation, a club, a gang, a profession - or whether we believe that we are born with a cluster of molecules in our brains which have evolved through natural selection over thousands of years to enable us to have this experience and deal with it. If we find the theories contradict each other, this has more to do with our limited ways of thinking than with the nature of archetype. If we insist on imaging archetypes as 'things', it is easy enough to argue that there is no evidence that such 'things' exist. On the other hand, if we give up thinking of the universe as comprised of 'things' and imagine it rather as an emerging process, we see archetypal patterning as an aspect of this process.[7]

One philosopher, a contemporary of Jung, who understood the world as emerging process was Alfred North Whitehead. His theory of 'eternal objects' in some respects parallels Jung's theory of archetypes. Their understanding differs in that Jung' archetypes are pre-existing patterns which shape our behaviour. They come out of the past and drive us forward. In contrast, Whitehead's eternal objects are potentialities which draw us towards the future. Every moment is a moment of creativity in which we and the world are drawn towards eternal potentialities such as beauty, harmony and peace. In each moment we choose either to repeat our past or create our future, taking a step towards the realization of our, and the world's, potential. We should note that Whitehead's eternal objects, like Jung's archetypes, are not "things" which exist independent of our experience. They only exist in their manifestations in our individual and collective behaviour, human and non-human. They exist in our becoming, not in our being. Giving archetypal patterns the names of Greek gods (as people in the European classical world and the European renaissance did) brings our capacity for poetry into the service of our understanding. We can, if we like, believe in the gods as brings our capacity for poetry into the service of our understanding. We can, if we like, believe in the gods as transcendent persons, but this is theology, not psychology. The question whether divinity is best imagined as singular or plural is certainly worth asking, but it is not the question asked by archetypal psychologists. They are more interested in exploring the narratives of the gods for insights into human behaviour and culture. They look for the gods in our personalities and in the way we live our lives. It leads them to a pluralistic understanding of values.

If we take the lead from archetypal psychology, the Greek pantheon can provide us with a language for talking about a wide range of distinct philosophies, value systems, energies, feeling states, habits of behaviour and political ideologies. It enables us to avoid accepting a single perspective on the climate crisis or the COVID19 crisis and our psychological response to them as representing the whole truth about these phenomena. The gods are many, and if we follow the advice of the ancient Greeks we will be careful not to neglect any of them - and not get too carried away in worshipping any single one of them, lest we manifest their pathology and suffer the vengeance of all the gods whom we neglect.

It is worth noting that the ancient Greeks understood that the gods are not constrained by our human notions of morality. From our point of view, it appears that there is both a healthy Zeus and a pathological Zeus, a benevolent Zeus and a vengeful Zeus. Ares energy manifests itself both in the mindless cruelty of battle and the passion which drives us to act in the world. Hermes is both the friendliest of the gods and the prince of liars. Demeter both mothers and smothers. In a Jungian frame work archetypal energies are morally neutral, having both a positive pole and a negative pole.

The following archetypal analysis is based on the situation in Australia at the time of writing, but I believe it has broader application.

Great Zeus

Every god has his or her stories. We mere mortals are caught up in them. Their myths were not invented but experienced. The way our culture has evolved we find that we are most powerfully caught up in the story of Zeus.

Zeus is the original Indo-European sky-god. His worship came to Greece with the waves of horse-riding cattle-herders who entered the Balkan Peninsula after 2000 B.C. As the Greek invaders established their political domination, he became the personification of patriarchal power in the family, in the clan and in the emerging city-states. We find him first depicted as a punitive and unpredictable weather-god, the Cloud-gatherer who sends hail, thunder and lightning. Later he came to be seen as to an all-powerful creator and a benevolent and wise father of humanity 'in whom we live, and move, and have our being'[8]. Later still, we find him representing (for the philosophers at least) the notion of pure, eternal, all-embracing divinity. He is the same sky-father as is worshipped in the Judaic-Christian-Islamic tradition.

The archetypal pattern personified in Zeus and manifested in human history and individual psychology is the pattern of power, the power which brings order to chaos, the power which maintains itself either brutally or benevolently, the power which can both protect and punish, the power which provides security as well as fear. Human beings generally prefer order, even autocratic order, to chaos. Zeus' ability to take command and give clear directions is often essential to our psychological health or to our safety. We may find this Zeus-energy within ourselves or we may project it onto someone else who is ready to take advantage of our compliance.

Nevertheless, Zeus is not omnipotent. When the Olympian gods managed to defeat the Titans and take control of the world, the Titan Prometheus, who had assisted the gods in their victory, expected to be rewarded by Zeus. When Zeus refused, Prometheus responded by creating men, who took over the Earth which the gods had expected to enjoy without interference. Zeus attempted many times to annihilate the race of men but they were saved by Prometheus, who brought them science and technology. They survived to be a source of irritation to Zeus.

When it comes to facing the corona virus we may well decide that strong global leadership provides the only escape from catastrophe. If our personal pathology leans in that direction, we may even decide to tolerate dictatorship, even global dictatorship, if that's the only way our species can survive. We may deny our own power, our own capacity to act, project our power onto an authoritarian leader and wait for rescue, hopefully before it is too late. In Australia, we have recently witnessed the unprecedented suspension of parliament for several months, with little public outrage at the abandonment of democratic process. The COVID19 crisis seems to be demanding what is conventionally referred to as 'strong leadership'. However we may reasonably be concerned that it is also contributing to a phenomenon which is already manifest - a global inflation of the Zeus archetype, observed in the deterioration of democracy and the increasing power of people described by Noam Chomsky as 'sociopathic buffoons'. Our national leadership is convinced that an authoritarian, even punitive, approach is necessary for the survival of our society.

There is certainly plenty of historical evidence witnessing the capacity of Zeus to successfully handle emergencies. However, we may have reason to fear that national leaders who successfully negotiate this crisis will take the opportunity to manifest a pathological Zeus, an authoritarian, punitive political stance which claims omnipotence and omniscience and tolerates no opposition.

Zeus eventually punished Prometheus for saving humans from extermination by chaining him to a rock at the far edge of the universe and sending his eagle each day to devour his liver. This punishment finally ended when Hermes persuaded Prometheus to tell Zeus the secret of how to maintain his power forever, the secret being that to maintain his power he must share it with the other gods. So Prometheus entered the pantheon and was worshipped as the god of science and technology, and we can see Zeus currently depending on him to end the plague by developing a vaccine.

In the current context, we can also see Zeus relying on other members of the Olympian family to preserve and exercise his power. Accordingly, we can look beyond Zeus' personality to the relationships between Zeus and the other gods for further insights into the complex patterns which shape our behaviour. The relationship between Zeus and Hera is manifest in the connection between authority and societal stability. The patriarchy's inclination to either seduce or rape the feminine is found in the relationship between Zeus and Aphrodite. Zeus and Hermes concocted the global financial crisis. A stable authoritarian system depends on Apollo for its structures. It is Eros who binds the patriarch to his family and determines whether his company's culture is toxic or creative. And so on. The familial and erotic

11

relationships between the gods is as significant a factor in shaping our behaviour as the gods' individual personalities.

Archetypal psychologists, following James Hillman, commonly refer to the Senex (old man) archetype. This term applies to the pre-Olympian Greco-Roman gods: Uranus, Kronos, Saturn. In the Olympian pantheon, Zeus and his brothers Hades and Poseidon point to the same values: patriarchal power, conservatism, attachment to tradition. Their influence is countered by the Puer (child/adolescent) gods, Eros, Hermes and Dionysus, who represent our yearning for change and creative expression. We find the tension between Senex and Puer in our individual experience and in our society.

Glorious Hera

It is conventional enough to think of the desire for power as instinctual, or to see power as a value or perspective which may dominate some people's thinking and behaviour. We are inclined to imagine power as top-down, as personified in Zeus, the sky- god, but there is another kind of power, personified in Zeus' consort, Hera.

Hera, for the classical Greeks, was the Queen who shared in the power of King Zeus, the Wife who remained loyally in the background while the divine Husband attended to the affairs of the universe, and who jealously guarded her special status in the face of Zeus' inclination to pursue other goddesses and mortals. There are indications in the myths that she was a mighty goddess in the Balkan peninsula long before Zeus was thought of, and that the sacred marriage of Zeus and Hera represents the need of the Indo-European invaders to domesticate her. She, like other goddesses in the Olympian family, is a manifestation of the Great Mother, Gaia, from whose womb we are born and to whom we return. Her power is the power of the earthbound matriarchal culture which was overrun by the sky-worshipping invaders from the North. Her power is the horizontal power of tribal relationship, not the hierarchical power of Big Daddy in the Sky.

After her incorporation into the patriarchal cult she retained vestiges of this. She is goddess of family, of social obligations, of the bonds of blood and the bonds of commitment, loyalty and fidelity which unite people. In the exercise of her power she supports the authority of Zeus. We currently see our political leadership calling on our sense of obligation to family and society to motivate us, and decrying the social irresponsibility of those who do not observe the regulations they have imposed.

Hera is a great and glorious goddess who is capable of extraordinary pettiness and spite. She sometimes appears as an old woman, for she represents the wisdom of the old ways. She is more often represented as a mature and fulfilled woman, who can occasionally bend even Zeus to her will.

In the Greek imagination, Hera represents social stability. Homer and the other poets depict her as the god of all those familial and social bonds and shared expectations which keep a society from exploding into fragments. To use the language of *image schemas* her behaviour is shaped to the pattern of *containment* and *force*. The container of society, the container of shared values, the container of loyalty and responsibility, all function as a means of control - on behalf of Zeus. The easy exercise of authority depends on having a stable society. Hera abhors change. She attaches no value to creativity or personal growth. Her priorities are responsibility, loyalty, respect, commitment, honour, stability, dignity. She has her own religious language and her own religious rituals. She is jealous of her relationship with Zeus, and always does her work with his interests in mind.

There is no place in Hera's world for individuals who give priority to their own satisfaction and personal fulfilment. Every member of a family or other group (including 'team Australia') must put commitment and loyalty ahead of personal whims and satisfactions. It is important to the stability of the social group that all its members know their roles and responsibilities and carry them out. Our political leadership is currently rediscovering our dependence on these Hera-values. Conservative politicians who were once blinded by a Thatcherite ideology which proclaimed that 'there is no such thing as society' and the belief that people must look after themselves first of all, are reminding the voters of the need to look after each other, to isolate themselves not merely for self-protection but for the protection of the whole community.

Herakles And Dionysus, The Hero And The Hedonist

Herakles and Dionysus are sons of two of Zeus' human lovers. Hera, jealous wife as she is, is naturally antagonistic to them, though they both survived her persecution to eventually attain divinity. However, the goddess of the family has little tolerance for gods who subvert social stability.

These two represent two very different versions of what it means to be an individual, but both are in conflict with Hera values. For Hera, the notion of individual growth (Dionysus) is as meaningless as the notion of the individual struggle (Herakles).

Both Herakles and Dionysus are young gods. Their stories are largely stories of adolescent adventure. In Greek myth and legend both heroism and hedonism are associated with youth. We note that the current community transmission of COVID19 seems to be associated in large part with young adults either insisting on their right to have fun or resisting the directive to wear masks and keep physical distance from each other. Risk-taking is an aspect of adolescence; it is also an aspect of heroism.

Individuals who are driven by Herakles-energy insist on their right-to-be-me-and-to-do-my-own-thing and accordingly insist that the isolation regulations should not apply to them. Herakles (the Roman Hercules) was the superhero of the classical world, strong, courageous and not terribly bright, energetically helping people but sometimes inadvertently leaving a trail of destruction behind him.

There has been a good deal of hero-talk during the current crisis. The authorities keep referring to the heroism of health professionals and the hospital workers supporting them. Putting aside any cynicism about politicians who are living in comfortable safety wanting to motivate low-paid workers to keep doing what we need them to do, we must acknowledge that there is a capacity (tendency? instinct?) sometimes manifested in human beings to sacrifice their wellbeing and risk their lives to help people for whom they have no obvious responsibility. Heroism turns up in unlikely places.

Heroic behaviour is grounded in personal choice, irrespective of family or other societal obligations which might shape it. We are immersed in the Hero fantasy and engage with our Hero energy whenever we exercise our right to make a personal choice which might not be approved by others.

People who refuse to comply with the authoritarian demand that they isolate themselves during the plague, may imagine that their non-compliance represents a courageous assertion of their independence. In the protests inspired by the Black Lives Matter movement we see Herakles at work opposing Zeus, who hates not being in control, and Hera, who regards such movements as socially irresponsible. We can see the presence of Eros in the sense of community experienced by the protesters, and Hestia in their sense of belonging to a movement which defines them. When we look at the violence sometimes associated with these protests we can see both Ares' justifiable rage at centuries of oppression and Hermes' collusion with pathological Ares to engage in opportunistic criminal attacks on people and property.

In the world of COVID19 some people refuse to wear face masks. It may not seem a particularly heroic thing to do, but in its essence, it is a manifestation of the Hero archetype. It belongs with Lucifer's cry of 'I will not serve', Luther's declaration: 'Here I stand. I can do no other' and teenagers' efforts to separate themselves from their parents. For an archetypal psychologist or a structuralist philosopher, it is not simply the free choice of an individual spirit but the expression of a deep structure in which their lives are embedded and their culture supports.

Dionysus is equally subversive of proper social values. The worship of Dionysus seems to have had two sources. On the one hand, he was the divine child, the son of the indigenous Earth

Mother, representing, new life, fertility, creativity. On the other hand, he seems to have arrived from Western Asia as a god of drunkenness and religious ecstasy. The authorities found his worship somewhat unsettling and did not at first approve of it. Here was a god to be worshipped through mystical rites, whose followers sought ecstatic communion with him, who ran enthusiastically into the mountains to give themselves over to madness and orgiastic celebrations. The authorities are still suspicious of Dionysus, and acknowledge him very reluctantly. He is the god of go-with-the-flow and do-my-own-thing. He brings both joy and grief. He is the god of the adrenaline charge, the god of tragedy, of feeling, of impulse, of play, of suffering, of exhilaration, of charisma, of performance, of ecstasy, of newness, of freedom, of flow, of spontaneity. He is the god of the significant minority of people who are outraged by the regulations which prohibit them from risking their health and society's control of the virus by meeting to drink and party.

He is the god also of those who work in the creative arts and who are convinced that the closing of theatres and galleries means the end of civilization. Nevertheless we can see the Dionysus energy driving the Arts community to find new ways to express their creativity. Furthermore, many people outside the artistic community have recently found Dionysus within themselves and have got in touch with a need for creative expression which had previously gone unacknowledged.

We are inclined to associate creativity primarily with the Arts and while we may acknowledge its impact in other fields like science, economics and politics, we are somewhat risk-averse when it comes to supporting developments in such areas. The Australian government may be reluctant to give support to the Arts, but we note that the compulsory closure of the retail industry made an exception for bottle-shops. We also note that bottle-shops are doing an exceptionally brisk trade at the moment, and both men and women are drinking more alcohol. Dionysus, for better and for worse, is alive and well in the age of corona.

We are inclined to think that creativity is something we have, an add-on to supplement the other personality traits we are born with or develop. For an archetypal theorist, this is profoundly wrong.

Creativity has us. It pre-exists us and continues to exist after we are gone. For a process thinker like Whitehead creativity is the very core of the universe's being. The physical world is not composed of inert matter which has somehow accumulated properties such as life and creativity. Life comes first. Creativity is life's essential quality. The physical universe is just a way that life manifests itself. The creativity at the centre of our being involves us, if we let it, in what Whitehead calls the 'creative advance' of the universe.

We should note that in the current Australian situation neither Herakles-driven or Dionysus-driven individuals are making much impact on proceedings. In Australia, the relatively low incidence of infection can be attributed to the population generally complying with government demands on their behaviour. In spite of Australians' cherished self-image as rugged individualists, even larrikins, it seems that more than some other nations they have a strong tendency to do as they are told.

Hades: The End And The Beginning

The Greeks had two narratives of Hades, god of the Underworld. Sometimes they saw him as our final end, the god who collects us when our life is over, a god who we don't waste our time worshipping because there's nothing he will do for us. Our one- way trip to Hades and eternal boredom is inevitable and inescapable. On the other hand, in some of their rituals they identified him with Dionysus, the god of new life.

Freud distinguished two great forces which he labelled Eros and Thanatos, and in our conventional ways of thinking we tend to imagine Life and Death to be opposites. Not so in many other cultures. For them, life and Death are the same phenomenon, looked at from different perspectives. We only stay alive because our cells are constantly dying and being replaced. We cannot avoid the image of Death in our current crisis, but we hang onto the hope of rebirth, if not for ourselves personally but at least for our society. Our politicians assure us that when this version of the plague has gone our society will be reborn. They even use the Dionysian image of growth to describe what this will be like. Unfortunately, we have to remember that it is our greed-driven growth (Hades is the god of Greed) which is rushing us towards the death of our species.

In the world of COVID19 Hades' presence is hard to avoid.

Existential philosophers are inclined to label our fear of Death as a core existential anxiety. However, we can argue, as Schopenhauer did[9], that this fear is based on the delusional assumption that our personal, continuing existence in the world is somehow important. In the greater scheme of things my continuing existence, and yours, is of very little significance. I am not the centre of the cosmos, and neither are you. Neither is our society or our species. We come and go and life goes on. Life is not something we have. Life is prior to us and we are simply temporary manifestations of it.

We find both aspects of Hades in our fears and expectations of the kind of society which will emerge after the plague. On the one hand we see the opportunity for a Dionysian transformation, a new society, a new economics, a new culture. On the other we hear our politicians talking of returning to 'normal', by which they mean the dysfunctional system to which we have been accustomed. Inertia is one of the most powerful forces in the universe, and it is personified in Hades.

Mother Demeter

Jung found that the image of mother as container is universal in human experience, and that it is psychologically significant. When he looked to mythology and religious belief he could find stories of the Mother Goddess which matched the observations that he and Freud had made about our infantile attachment to mother and the conflict between our need to escape from mother's embrace and our need to remain in it.

The Great Mother of Greek mythology has many names - Ge (Gaia), Rhea, Themis, Maia, Cybele. She is the primeval womb from which we all come, the primeval breast which continues to nourish us. Primal humans had no sense of themselves as distinct from the earth, just as infants have no sense of themselves as being distinct from their mother. The evolution of rational consciousness broke our union with the earth, and we have been suffering the loss ever since.

Mother Earth has been nourishing us humans for millennia and instead of thanking her we have caused her a lot of damage and are coming close to destroying her. James Lovelock writes of the revenge of Gaia,[10] with a focus on environmental catastrophe, caused by the over-exploitation of her gifts and the invisible toxins we have created. We have not yet discovered a clear connection between the relationship of humans to the earth and the emergence of COVID19, but it is highly likely that such connection will eventually become apparent. In the mean time we can contemplate the possibility that we are here experiencing the revenge of Gaia. Or perhaps this plague is what the great organism we call Mother Earth must do to protect herself against the pain which we, her ungrateful children, inflict on her. If we want to use the language of science rather than the language of mythology we can point out COVID19 and human beings are equally elements of an ecological system in which everything is connected. Disturbance at one point is experienced through the whole system. Unfortunately, disturbance is what humans do.

The different goddesses of the Greek pantheon represent different aspects of Gaia. Demeter was worshipped both as goddess of the harvest and goddess of human mothering. There is clearly a pattern in human affairs which we call mothering, and Demeter personifies it. She gives birth, she suckles, she provides, she is anxious for her child, she grieves, she gives her child the love and support necessary for growth. This is a psychological pattern as well as a biological one, and men as well as women share in it.

One thing which has invaded our consciousness since the arrival of coronavirus is the critical importance of nursing in maintaining the health, even the survival, of our society. Nursing is a profession where mothering skills are often needed. Nurses with strong Demeter values take mothering seriously. Central to their image of themselves is their task of providing a safe and supportive environment for their patients. They are currently risking their health, even their lives, in taking on the task of caring for the afflicted. They take responsibility for the care of their patients exercising the role of the carer and nourisher, balancing the roles of doctors who may be Zeus-like in their power and status, Apollo-like in their dedication to science, or Hestia-like in their determination to serve the community.

There is currently considerable public outrage at the revelation that aged care facilities in this country have largely abandoned Demeter and failed to exercise the care expected of them. The outrage of families who have lost grandparents to COVID19 after entrusting them to these facilities is often exacerbated by a Hera-fuelled ambivalence about entrusting them to strangers in the first place.

It has been argued very plausibly that for a century or more we have been experiencing a gradual shift from a patristic to a matristic society. The grounds for this argument have been drawn from many fields and the argument has by no means been confined to feminist writing. There is a sense that the growth of feminism and the growth of the ecological movement are aspects of the same phenomenon. Many people at the beginning of the twenty-first century are energized by the conviction that the future, if there is to be a future at all, must belong to Gaia/Demeter.[11]

One manifestation of the Mother archetype is our desire to be mothered, to be looked after. Governments whose ideology is vehemently opposed to welfare are now responding to the public demand to be looked after. Abandoning their conviction that individuals are responsible for their own economic circumstances and that the population can be divided into 'lifters and leaners' our national leadership is extending welfare in ways which, if the political opposition had proposed it, would have drawn their contempt. And we find billionaire businessmen who previously boasted that their wealth and success was the product of their individual acumen and energy, seeking to be looked after by the Mother State.

From a Jungian perspective, we seem to be witnessing, both in the conservative and neo-liberal politicians who are embracing the welfare state and their supporters who welcome it, the phenomenon of *enantiadromia* - the sudden shift from one psychological state to its opposite. We might suppose that extreme circumstances have now enabled their repressed need to mother and be mothered to emerge, however they may rationalize this change.

Freud must take some of the blame for the fact that it is socially approved to blame our mothers for everything we don't like about ourselves. Even many feminists have colluded with the patriarchy in ridiculing motherhood. We can see readily enough the negative aspects of the goddess in Demeter-inflated teachers, nurses, social workers or counsellors. We see dependence, possessiveness, vicarious living, neediness, the manipulation of affection. However, awareness of Demeter's pathology should not leave us unable to acknowledge the positive Demeter aspects - nurturance, protection, sacrifice, love - while acknowledging the dangers of leaving it all to Mother.

Bright-Eyed Athena

When the Sky-god arrived in Greece, he brought with him his warrior-daughter, whom people variously called Kore, Parthenos or Pallas, all of which simply mean the Girl. There was already a Girl-goddess worshipped in Greece, who was in some places called Athena. She was a sort of 'palace goddess', of Cretan origin[12], responsible for protecting the peace and good order of the royal household, a goddess of practical wisdom and practical crafts. Since the Greek invaders happily adopted the gods of the conquered peoples rather than suppress their worship, these two goddesses were readily identified as one. As Pallas Athena, she became the protector-goddess of the city-states, especially of the city-state of Athens, where her worship was most enthusiastic.

With the development of both democracy and imperialism in fifth century Athens she became, for the Athenians at least, the symbol of both. In late classical times, she became the personification of wisdom, and stayed on in Christian times as Sophia, the Wisdom of God.

There is plenty of evidence in art and poetry that the ancient Greeks were deeply devoted to Athena. They told of her birth from the brow of Zeus, of her competing with Hera and Aphrodite in the divine beauty contest judged by the Trojan prince Paris, of her patronage of heroes like Odysseus, Jason, Herakles and Perseus, whom she assisted in their various adventures. They told of her help to those engaged in crafts, and her vindictive punishment of human women like Medusa and Arachne, who claimed to rival her beauty or skill.

Since Athena is the assimilation of the patriarchal daughter with one of the manifestations of the Great Goddess she represents a point where sky-worship meets earth-worship, where masculine meets feminine, where abstract culture meets concrete culture, where vertical power structures meet horizontal ones. She is, then, the goddess of balance, of normality, of common sense. Unlike the numerous gods of the bizarre, who manage to make our lives exciting, Athene represents our instinct for the normal, our tendency to avoid extremes. She is a goddess with attributes which we are now inclined to stereotype as masculine. She is, for instance, a god of war. Not vehement, sword-wielding, blood- lusting warfare, waged for the violence and the glory of it (like Ares, the other Olympian war god), but cool, intelligent, calculating, strategic warfare, waged to defend one's city and citizens. She is also a god of peace, and of the civilized living that comes with peace. She teaches us the arts and sciences which form the basis of this civilization. She also teaches us that we must fight to defend them. She is the goddess of cooperation and the democratic process. Yet she has little interest in relationships, except in so far as they have strategic value.

Athena hopefully manifests herself in our capacity to take a balanced approach to crisis. She abhors alarmism and panic and insists that we weigh up evidence, consult and cooperate with our associates and attempt to reach a reasonable consensus. In our current emergency, she offers an alternative approach to the top- down, authoritarian decision-making favoured by many national leaders and proposed as the only way disaster can be averted. When authoritarian leaders argue that democratic structures are incapable of delivering the tough strategies which are essential if the crisis is to be averted, they are referring to pathological Athena, where the desire to take everybody's opinion into consideration makes effective decision-making impossible. On other hand, Zeus' tendency to make decisions based on his conviction that he is always right, and that other peoples' opinions are irrelevant, leads to lamentable decisions.

In the current Australian context, we can hear Zeus employing his daughter Athena's rhetoric of cooperation and consultation strategically, while hanging on to his assumption that his decisions are always correct, professing to listen to all relevant voices while excluding the voices which might disagree with his decisions. The early rhetoric of cooperation between federal and state governments is no longer convincing, and the relationship between Prime Minister and Premiers is fracturing.

In the current context, Father and Daughter seem to be in a somewhat uneasy relationship. In the Athena style of administration decisions are made coolly and sensibly, after full debate, with full attention to practical implications. The preferred way of developing strategies for dealing with problems is a collaborative approach that recognizes and utilizes people's different kinds of expertise. Too much emotionality is frowned on. Athena may represent the independent, resourceful, clear- sighted feminine, but she accepts the ground-rules laid down by Zeus. She is prepared to work in a men's world.

In Australia and New Zealand, we are fortunate that the Athena instinct in our national character is strong enough to ensure that our national leaders and their advisors present an image of reasonableness and moderation. This is in contrast to the Zeus pathology we witness in some other places, where the Mad Emperor brooks no limits to his narcissism.

It is clear that Athena is currently supporting Zeus, but if the rhetoric of reasonableness and cooperation does not achieve the desired result Zeus will have no hesitation in moving into his punitive mode.

Shining Apollo

Like Athena, Apollo seems to be an assimilation of two similar de-ities. There is one line of evidence which points to an origin in Asia, and his central myth makes him the child of Leto (a personification of the Great Mother) and another which suggests that he was an In-do-European god who entered Greece with the invading Dorians13. There were actually two distinct cults of Apollo, one centred in the Aegean island of Delos, and the other in the mountain shrine of Del-phi on the mainland, where Apollo spoke through his oracle. In addi-tion, there was a tendency to identify him with Helios, the sun, and by Roman times this identification was complete. It is Apollo Helios who makes all things visible, who lays bare the truth.

Whatever his origins, he became a thoroughly Greek god, the eldest son of Zeus, the symbol of what it meant to be Greek and civilized: art, music, science, poetry, physical and moral beauty, respect for law, medicine, athletic prowess and a sense of moderation. In the Greek theatre, we find the impulsivity and spontaneity of Dionysus moder-ated by Apollo's concern for rules. The creativity of the Greek dra-matist functioned within fairly rigid structures, just as standard forms such as the sonnet and the sonata have been the vehicle for creative masterpieces. The Greeks were suspicious of Dionysus' potential for damage. Then as now, the influence of Apollo is needed to prevent us from mistaking our unconstrained impulses for creative expression.

The eldest son of the Father is a very masculine, even misogynist, god. In the patriarchal culture of Europe culture was generally assumed to be an entirely masculine domain. (The Muses, who provided the inspiration, were obviously feminine, but the practitioners were usually men,) Apollo was, besides, the god of prophecy and healing. However, the myth of Apollo shows him to be very inept when it comes to relationships.

Like Athena, Apollo is sometimes able to moderate the impulsive, unpredictable, self-aggrandizing behaviour of his father Zeus, who has little respect for law and rationality. We are currently seeing national leaders making impulsive pronouncements and then being brought back to more moderate and reasonable positions by their advisors. When politicians move into positions of power they are inclined to regard the law as an inconvenience, and will ignore it if they can. If our Apollo instincts are strong enough we will insist that they are within the law, not outside it. It is the Apollo in us, also, that causes us to be anxious when our leaders' approach to the crisis is contradictory or ambiguous. We want to know what is what, we want certainty and clarity and count on Apollo to provide them. When the leadership claims that flexibility is more useful than certainty at the moment (homage to Hermes) they may well be right, but that does not satisfy people in whom the archetypal energy of Apollo is strong.

Where reason is not honoured, Apollo appears in the form of rationalizations and rationalisms of various kinds. When we cease to respect our sense that reason can guide us towards truth, we find ourselves in a groundlessness which some people escape by embracing dogma or magic. We are currently seeing politicians and journalists who have been busy dismissing the expertise of scientists who address the issue of global warming, declaring it to be 'simply opinion', suddenly reversing their attitude to scientific expertise and declaring the critical importance of medical science. We can only wonder whether their respect for science will outlast the pandemic when they must again confront the much greater crisis of a warming planet. For the past couple of decades our national leaders have shown little respect for Apollo and little appreciation of his domains, the Arts or the Sciences. The generous subsidies offered by the Australian government for currently struggling industries don't extend to the Apollo domains of Arts and Science. We must admit that Apollo has rarely been adequately honoured by Australian governments and, indeed, has been seriously neglected for the past decade. We no longer have ministries of the Arts and Science and funding in these areas is minimal. Both the Arts and Sciences focus on discovering and manifesting the truth, and the truth is currently not much valued by those in power.

It is the Apollo within us and within our culture that urges us to seek truth and beauty, but his pathology emerges in a tendency to dogmatism and rigidity. Apollo-inflated leaders (and scientists) are inclined to insist that the people accept their assessment of a situation, because its reasonableness is perfectly clear to them and those who can't see this must be stupid or bloody-minded. They are blind to the critical influence of emotions, relationships and unconscious drives on people's behaviour, and sometimes make bad decisions because this perspective prevents them from taking in certain kinds of information. They mistake their individual perspective for a universal truth.

It is some decades since Jurgen Habermas pointed out flaws in the notion of rationality we have inherited from the enlightenment.[14] Truth is only accessible through individual human intelligence and individual human intelligences will inevitably use logic to arrive at entirely different versions of the truth. Habermas observed that while truth can potentially be approached through open dialogue between the different perspectives, it is more likely to be neglected altogether. When we hear political authority telling us the truth about a phenomenon such as COVID19 and what it means for us, we need to note that it is not much interested in some kind of objective truth. It is much more interested in selling us an idea. It is not Apollo, the god of truth we can hear, but his brother Hermes, god of disguise, god of the marketplace and god of spin.

For the Zeus-inflated politician truth is whatever he or she decides it is. For Apollo, truth is what the evidence and rational thinking declares it to be. In the global crisis, we can see a clear contrast between national leaders whose Zeus energy is tempered by their respect for Apollo's gifts of reason, law and structure, (and Athena's gifts of balance, cooperation and consultation) and the Mad Emperors in USA, Brazil, Belarus and elsewhere who appear to be possessed by a Zeus pathology.

It is significant that on the one hand such Zeus-inflated leaders such as Trump and Putin depend on law and stable institutions (Apollo's domain) to establish and maintain their authority, but subvert these same laws and institutions when it appears that they might challenge their power.

Apollo shares with his sister Athena a lack of interest in relationships. The idea that self-imposed or law-imposed isolation should be seen as a burden or a punishment is foreign to the Apollo perspective. In this perspective, isolation is valued as an opportunity to do one's best work.

Since Freud and his friends started telling us what is wrong with us, we have tended to assume that solitary thinkers must be miserable. We have been told that we need to have lots of friends and be in an intimate relationship to be happy. Indeed, some still argue that humans can neither be happy nor healthy unless they are in a satisfying sexual relationship. History appears to say otherwise.

Many of the great achievements in European arts, philosophy and science have been the work of men who were single, celibate and solitary. (The achievements of women tended to be ignored or attributed to men.) Some of these men even appear to have led satisfying lives.15 The hermit in the silence of the mountain or desert, the philosopher in his library, the sculptor in his studio and the scientist in his laboratory, have been driven by Apollo energy in their quest for understanding and beauty. In an Apollo mode of apprehension, beauty is perceived to be experienced by our intelligence, not by our feeling. Nature as discovered by science is beautiful, whether or not we feel it to be so, and the scientist's mission is articulate this beauty, often finding mathematical symbols a more valid means of expression than mere words.

We should note that Apollo is god not only of the Sciences but of the Arts, especially music, the most abstract of the Arts. Here we find the intersection between the divine force we call Apollo

(Reason) and the divine force we call Beauty (Aphrodite). To cite Whitehead:

> *The scientist does not study nature because it is useful to do so. He studies it because he takes pleasure in it; and he takes pleasure in it because it is beautiful. If nature were not beautiful, it would not be worth knowing and life would not be worth living. I mean the intimate beauty which comes from the harmonious order of its parts and which a pure intelligence can grasp.*[16]

To cite Whitehead again, it is the lure of beauty which stimulates us emerge from our past and create ourselves anew.

Golden-Haired Aphrodite

In recent years, we have seen the strange phenomenon of people, especially young people, apparently valuing the relationships available on their mobile phones over the relationships available to them face to face. Stereotypically we see a group of people sitting around a table at a café, carrying on a desultory conversation while their true commitment is to the messages on their phone screens. The isolation imposed by COVID19 has shown us the inadequacy of such an approach to relationship. The inability to relate flesh to flesh, to see, hear, smell and touch one another, leaves most of us unsatisfied. Our Apollo-need is for abstraction and meaning. Other gods drive our need for hugs.

Aphrodite, for the Greeks of classical times, and for European culture ever since, is the goddess of beauty and sensuality. She is overtly and unselfconsciously sexual, the only goddess who appears naked to mortals. She believes in fun, in immediate gratification, in the ultimate power of Beauty. She has none of Hera's concern for respectability and social obligations, none of Apollo's interest in ideas or concern for the Law. She is irresponsible and self-indulgent, careless of the consequences of her actions. Jung reminds us that the archetypes have both positive and negative poles. We can find Aphrodite in romantic love and also in violent pornography, where the pathology of Aphrodite and her lover, Ares, join forces.

When we consider that, in classical Greece, Aphrodite was perhaps the most popular of all the gods, it is interesting to note that she was a foreigner. She is a Greek version of the Great Goddess of Western Asia. It was probably through Cyprus that the worship of this Semitic mother-goddess made its way to Greece, for the most popular story of her origin has her emerging from the sea near that island, having sprung from the foam around the genitals of the old god Uranus when his son Kronos sliced them off and cast them in the sea. The Greek-Phoenician culture of Cyprus began Aphrodite's transformation from a fertility goddess to a goddess of beauty and pleasure. In classical Greece and in European culture since then she is Beauty personified, whose particular domain is sexual attraction. She gets plenty of attention in popular culture, but she does not get much mention in political discourse.

From a Freudian perspective, she represents libido. One of Freud's key notions is that it is sexual energy which drives most of human behaviour. This implies, among other thing, that all relationships, with people or with things, are grounded in erotic attraction. Greek mythology expresses the same insight, for the myth of Aphrodite makes her the mother of Eros, the god of relationship and love.

People living in an environment dominated by Aphrodite may pay a lot of attention to personal appearance; they may be obsessed with the need to be attractive; they may be more interested in the elegance of what they do than with its usefulness or efficiency; they may not have much interest in doing anything at all if it is not fun.

John Keats proclaimed the fantasy that:

> *Beauty is truth, truth beauty, that is all we know and all we need to know.*[17]

This is the perspective of Apollo, the other god of beauty, rather than that of Aphrodite. Aphrodite is not interested in truth. Her focus is the sensual experience associated with our engagement with beauty. Beauty in the world of Apollo is the beauty of a mathematical equation, the beauty of a scientific theory and the beauty of a Bach fugue. The scientist and the mathematician pursue their approximations of the truth and find their satisfactions in the 'rightness' of their discoveries. The same can be said of many literary, musical and visual artists. The 'lure of beauty' (Whitehead's term) leads them to the intellectual satisfaction of seeing the product of their work, knowing that it expresses something of the truth and finding it beautiful. Whitehead, who was an eminent mathematical physicist before he identified as a philosopher, was speaking out of his own experience when he declared that scientists are lured forward, moment by moment, by the urge towards beauty. His contemporary, Albert Einstein, expressed the same idea. According to Whitehead truth and beauty are directions toward which all science and art - and even the universe itself - are pointing. 'Science and art are the consciously determined pursuit of Truth and of Beauty.'[18]

Beauty is not an add-on, not a cosmetic improvement to an otherwise drab universe. Rather, in Whitehead's radical cosmology, it is the central purpose of the universe. The universe has a direction, and that direction is towards the production of beauty.

If we take Whitehead seriously we will observe that it is the 'lure of beauty' which constantly shapes our behaviour, whether we are aware of it or not. However, beauty is not only to be found through our cognition. Our satisfaction in 'getting it right', is grounded in another sort of satisfaction, the sensual and emotional satisfaction of finding ourselves in touch with beauty. The lure of beauty is felt in our bodies before we have any thoughts about it. This is Aphrodite's work. Whether we are using our compulsory isolation to produce a masterpiece, paint our bedroom, cook a meal, organize the pantry or tool shed or immerse ourselves in a landscape, we are submitting to the lure of beauty. Aphrodite is alive in us, even in our vaguest feelings. Whitehead writes about our need to 'attend to that physical reaction to the world which says with incorrigible definiteness, "This is important", "That is different", "This is lovely."[19]

We can see both Aphrodite and Apollo manifest as gods of beauty in the time of Corona. We see medical scientists and technicians seeking solutions which are not only functional but elegant; we see people taking advantage of their isolation to complete all the unfinished tasks which can make their dwelling satisfyingly complete; we see people who have rediscovered their creativity striving to make the products of their creativity as perfect as they can. I am aware in the midst of this writing that I intend to write until it approximates to some sort of truth, that I will write until I have a sense of completion, that I will choose my words for their sound as much as for their accuracy, that I will write until it 'feels right'. Drawn by the lure of beauty.

In the world according to Aphrodite, beauty provides our key motivation and shapes our behaviour. However, we should remember Whitehead's assertion that 'all truths are half-truths'. There are other gods whose truths must be acknowledged.

Winged Eros,

...unstrings the limbs and subdues both mind and sensible thought in the breasts of all gods and all men. [20]

The power of Eros is felt by humans and gods alike, in their propensity to fall obsessively in love. It is felt in both the delight and the anguish of intimacy. Eros is singularly the god of relationship, and of the creativity which is generated by relationship. Aphrodite may prompt our hugs, but it is Eros who creates the connection.

According to one tradition, Eros was the most ancient of the gods. It was Eros who brought Sky (Uranus) and Earth (Gaia) together to generate the gods, who presided over the unions of gods and mortals, who is ultimately the source of life. This personification of cosmic harmony was present at the birth of the gods and mortals and present also in their love-making, for love and the generation of life are obviously manifestations of the same god, the god of union, harmony and creativity.

Eros was originally the force which brings things together. In the pre-scientific mind the attraction between two people or the desire for a beautiful object or person was the same force as the gravity which draws things towards the earth and the magnetic attraction which draws certain objects towards magnetite or amber. When the Greeks of later times imagined this god, it was as an adolescent boy, for their experience of love included more than the simple drive to union. Eros, as they imagined him, was unpredictable and irresponsible and destructive as well as delightful and creative. Eros is firmly established in classical mythology and the European imagination as both the oldest of the gods and the youngest, as a god of union and communion, relationship, newness and process, romance and delusion, procreative power.

The Eros energy in us manifests itself in a desire for intimacy. This may be unacknowledged and repressed, acknowledged and suppressed, regulated or surrendered to. Intimacy gives us pleasure and inspires our creativity, but this does not mean that more intimacy is always better. The detached view of Apollo observes that excess intimacy can often lead to something nasty, to hatred or exploitation. The Greeks could have warned us not to worship any god obsessively. We have yet to see how this plays out in families unexpectedly thrown into intimate contact for months with no escape.

We recognise Eros fairly easily as the god of Love, and we know that he is distinct from his mother, the goddess of Beauty and Sensuality, and that it is somehow his love for Soul which separates him from Aphrodite. We know Eros most of all as a god of emotional attachment. Eros is at work in sexual involvement, in family relationship and in simple friendships. It is from Eros that we get the joy of being comfortably close to someone, of working side by side with someone, of being connected. He is at work in the shared experience of people who confront a problem together, or who play as a team, or who bond together to protest against what they see as unjustified government interference in their lives. He is present in the love that binds musicians to their music, mathematicians to their mathematics, teachers to their teaching. Without Eros, music, mathematics and teaching are dead and deadly. It is through Eros, also, that the gods themselves come together and through him that they are loving and creative.

Freud looked at life from an Eros-perspective and saw, for a time at least, only one instinct, a unidimensional and unidirectional sexual instinct which he called 'libido'. Lust and relationship are closely related. We know Eros is the child of Aphrodite. Freud's influence on our thinking is felt every time we use the word 'erotic' to denote the sexual in both its narrowest and broadest senses. He saw creativity and relationship as one, just as the Eros myths do. The drive towards life is a drive towards unity. This seems true enough on the level of biological reproduction, but we need to carry the metaphor to other levels as well. It is in the coming together of two (or more) elements, two personalities, two ideas, two cultures, that something new comes into being. We have heard a lot of Eros rhetoric in the official response to the CORONA-19 crisis. The slogan: "We're all in this together" is designed to promote social bonding, not merely social cooperation. There is some evidence in the Australian context that it is working, engaging with the Eros perspective that tells us that we are not self-centred individuals but relational beings. We are yet to discover whether being in this together produces something truly creative which lasts beyond the crisis.

Whitehead developed his cosmology against the background of quantum physics on the assumption that the nature of universe observed at the sub-atomic level must be the nature of the universe all the way through, including in human experience. In such a universe, there are no 'things', only events. We, and the rest of the universe exist as a succession of 'drops of experience'. He saw the sub-atomic particles of which we and the world consist emerging for a microsecond and disappearing. It is the web of connections within which they exist and the creative energy which drives the process which give the universe its stability. The universe is alive and relational. Whitehead called this living urge towards fulfilment 'the Divine Eros'.

At the human level, we find that we are essentially relational beings. None of us can exist independently of other humans. Nor can we exist independently of nonhuman beings. Like electrons and quarks, we emerge moment by moment from the web of relationships which constructs us.

The Greeks' experience of human loving may have prompted them to imagine Eros as a mischievous adolescent, and give him identity as the child of Aphrodite, or Artemis, or Zeus according to whatever aspect of his behaviour they were focusing on. However, beneath this mythologizing was the understanding that Eros was the most ancient of the gods, the creative force which prompted the emergence of the universe and gives it life. Eros, in both his cosmic and adolescent manifestations is present in all our reactions and interactions in the current crisis. Without Eros neither the Hera fantasy, the Apollo fantasy, the Athena fantasy or any of the others will enable us to find meaning and satisfaction in our experience. Whitehead merely confirmed what the ancient Greek theologians understood. It is love which makes the world go round.

Ares The Warrior

Aphrodite is married to Hephaistos, the god of work and crafting, who is obsessed with her but gets little in return. She gets her pleasure out of her affair with Ares, the war god.

We still see them together, in the appearance of scantily clad young women in the promotion of macho sports, in the tendency of sportsmen to partner with professional models, even in the attraction which some women appear to feel for violent men.

In the Greek pantheon, Ares would seem to have assured status as the only son of the marriage of Zeus and Hera. However, his parents don't seem to be particularly fond of him and the Greek people were suspicious of him. Homer makes him look somewhat ridiculous in his stories of how Ares was trapped in a net by Hephaistos while making love to Aphrodite, and of how he was beaten in battle by Athena (who detests him) and by the human hero Diomedes. His worship seems to have originated with the Thracians of Northern Greece, who were much fonder of war than the urbanized people of the South. As a war-god, Ares represents battle-fury, blood-lust, the exhilaration of conflict and conquest. This may have suited the Thracians, but most Greeks preferred to give their devotion to Athena, who personified intelligent, strategic warfare.

Ares is recognised easily enough in his negative aspect. The centuries are strewn with the consequences of Ares-pathology, both personal and tribal. We see his pathology in global aggression and soccer hooliganism, and we have good reason to be suspicious of him. However, Ares has a significant place in our lives. He is the god of energy, of vehemence, of conflict, of challenge, of activism, of fire in the belly and fire in the eyes. He is the exhilaration which some of us feel when engaged in competitive games, sports or commerce. If we are devotees of Athena, Eros or Hermes we are not likely to have much time for Ares. If we are religiously committed to the values of cooperation, relationship and dialogue, we are likely to see conflict and competition in an entirely negative light, and avoid giving them a place in our lives. However, we need to connect with our Ares energy if we are to be passionate about whatever is important to us.

It is Ares who provides the energy for passionate protest in the Black Lives Matter movement. It is not surprising that Ares energy also fuels the rage and anti-social violence which has sometimes attached itself to these protests.

We currently see national leaders everywhere using the language of Ares to persuade us to confront the pandemic with energy and focus. Their testosterone-driven rhetoric tells us that we are 'waging a war' on the virus, which is referred to as the 'invisible enemy', even 'a brilliant enemy'. There is regular reference to the two world wars as comparable events. Social distancing is an 'essential weapon in our arsenal'. Our courageous health workers are 'on the front line', 'in the line of fire' 'deep in the trenches', fighting a battle. Most importantly: 'We will never surrender'.

We find Ares also in the language of competition. As far as our political leadership is concerned it is not sufficient to be handling this crisis well. We have to be handling it better that other nations, especially New Zealand. The evidence that the New Zealand leadership has eliminated the virus in that country is countered by the claim that their approach has caused more damage to their economy than the approach taken by Australia. Obviously that makes us best, and everyone should admire and envy us.

We may well wonder whether war is the most appropriate metaphor in our imagining of the pandemic. We could as readily imagine it as a fire, a flood, a tsunami or an electrical storm. It is a matter of concern that the phenomenon of COVID19 is prompting people in some countries to buy more guns.

We must remember that both men and women are incomplete without Ares. To allow Ares to be undeveloped and unacknowledged in us is to risk having him run out of control. Even at his best he is not very smart. To deny him proper worship is to invite the emotional and physical violence which characterize his pathology.

Hermes The Cowboy

If there was any god more popular in classical times than Aphrodite, it was Hermes, the god of travellers, shepherds, thieves, merchants and scholars. It appears that the god known to the classical Greeks as Hermes was an amalgamation of several more ancient deities. There was a god who protected the flocks of the native peoples, and who lived in the stone-heaps they set up as boundary-markers. When the Greek invaders took their lands, the natives saw this god as their protector in whatever guerrilla activities they undertook to make life unpleasant for their oppressors. He became the god of thieving and trickery. The Cretans also, during their cultural domination of southern Greece, had introduced their own god of the stone-heap, the master of wild animals (and therefore protector of shepherds and travellers), who seems to have been a version of the earth-mother's son and consequently a god of fertility. The Greeks saw, naturally enough, that they were dealing with one god rather than two, and associated him also with trade, good luck, protection of the house, the supervision of boundaries, the bearing of messages from the gods and the conduct of the souls of the dead to the Underworld.

Like other Indo-European peoples, they already worshipped a god of trickery and magic[21], and readily identified him with this god of the conquered natives, making Hermes a very complex character.

The myth of Hermes, as recounted in the Homeric hymn in his honour, makes Hermes a very slippery character indeed. His slipperiness is reflected in the name the Romans gave him, Mercury, and in the image that his feet never touch the ground. He is an opportunist without any respect for conventional morality, a trickster, a liar and a thief. He is elusive, unpredictable and mischievous. He is also very charming. The Greeks believed him to be friendly to mortals, but they were careful not to trust him too much. He serves the needs of the patriarchy when it suits him, but is just as likely to subvert it. Even Zeus cannot trust him.

In recent years, the myth of progress (Prometheus' promise that technology would deliver prosperity, health and freedom) has been replaced by the myth of the marketplace, and Hermes, god of the marketplace, has taken a strong hold on our consciousness. For the last half century, the dominant political ideology has included with little question the dogma that the world's problems will be resolved by 'the magic hand of the marketplace'. Hermes is equally present in the casualization of labour, the commodification of higher education and the digitalization of our currency.

We have been expected to trust that events like the current pandemic would be prevented or contained by privatizing hospitals in Australia, reducing funding for the NHS in Britain, and attacking Obamacare in the US. We can now observe politicians putting on a caring expression to emphasize the need to care for the fragile and elderly but arguing energetically for the prime importance of supporting the economy. We find them very reluctant to attribute the dire condition of many aged care facilities to the privatization and commodification of the industry which they promoted and facilitated some years ago. We have even heard some of them proclaiming publicly that we must restore commercial operations as quickly as possible and that the deaths of countless elderly and fragile persons would be a small price to pay for releasing the marketplace from the current constraints.

Hermes is the Messenger, the god of information. He carries messages between the gods, and between gods and humans, without any concern as to whether the messages are true or not.

He is the god of spin, much more interested in appearance than reality. He has been powerful in Western culture for some decades. We have become used to politicians and business leaders lying to us and it appears that most of us no longer trust them. Spin has become conventional and can be observed every time a representative of the government submits to be questioned by an interviewer. We no longer expect an honest answer, even from politicians who argue the importance of transparency.

Hermes does not hold values of his own. He insists that we worship all the gods, including himself.

We are currently being informed that the current crisis forces us to be flexible and puts us 'beyond ideology'. Even a conservative politician like John Howard is talking like this. This is Hermes- talk. We saw the Hawke-Keating government go 'beyond ideology' when it embraced globalism and the unregulated marketplace in spite of the opposition of the protectionists and socialists in the Labour Party. They were doing Hermes work of dissolving boundaries. Now we see the Conservative coalition embracing protectionism and the welfare state, temporally at least, to the dismay of the neo-liberal and conservative ideologues on their side of politics. National boundaries, the domain of Hermes, have become critically important again.

Our current leaders may want us to believe that society will be fairer, more compassionate, more community-oriented, more egalitarian, more creative, more planet-conscious or whatever when this crisis is past, but we would do well to suspend our belief. Hermes may well be opportunistically talking on behalf of his father, Zeus, whose vision of the 'normal' to which we will return is of a society whose systems and processes are designed to preserve his power. In both Australia and the USA we see governments headed by personalities in whom Zeus and Hermes are in collusion. Scotty from marketing may well provide better leadership in this crisis than the Mad Emperor, but many of us have trouble trusting him. Even the tracking app, which seems to be a reasonable means of controlling the epidemic, is viewed with suspicion by many Australians who are happy to have their movements tracked by Facebook and Google but not by a government agency. Assurances that privacy will be respected are not enough. If they lied about other things why wouldn't they lie about this?

Nevertheless, it is Hermes who is the god of transitions and transformations. Because he believes in nothing in particular he is not stuck in any ideology. He is able to let go of a current set of certainties and take on another, and let go of that one when it suits him. This crisis is indeed an opportunity for change, but we need to make sure that it is not engineered by Zeus and his mates. It is a chance to stop repeating our past mistakes, to stop doing things the way we have always done them simply because this is the way we have always done them. It is a chance to listen to Dionysus, Eros and Athena.

When Maia, Hermes mother, who is a version of the Great Mother Gaia, suggests that his thieving and lying will get them both into trouble, his response is that 'I'm only doing it for you'.[22] If we take the myths seriously as articulations of cosmic patterns, this can give us hope that this crisis is a step towards planetary consciousness.

We need Hermes' gifts of flexibility, adaptability and imagination, even his opportunism and persuasiveness, to initiate change. In a world where we are told 'change is the only constant' a Hermes consciousness is essential. But in Health as in business, it must be balanced by the other gods or it will quickly bankrupt us. At the present time, the priority which our leaders are giving to the economy, and their assumption that they have only to release market forces to take us back to prosperity, leads us to fear that it is Hermes who will lead the recovery. When we hear that we are 'moving forward' to a more equal and compassionate society we should note that Hermes is the god of spin as well as the god of travellers. We would be well advised not to trust him too much.

The Gods Are Many

Jung suggested that there are a limited number of archetypes. The Greeks of classical times believed that the number of gods was not infinite, but was merely innumerable! James Hillman argued that everything is archetypal, suggesting that we are always within one archetype or another, a reminder that in archetypal theory we do not have the archetypes. They have us.[23]

In a full exposition of the mythical gods and their impact on our experience of COVID19 we need to include Artemis, the goddess of sisterhood and of wild nature. Unlike Athena and Hera, who are comfortable in a patriarchal world, she chooses a feminist alternative. As goddess of wild animals, she shares their natural grace, their ability to live in harmony with nature and their fierceness. There is evidence that the pandemic has its source in our failure to respect the needs of wild animals. Recent reports from the UN, the WHO and the WWF have pointed out that our destruction of wild places and the illegal wildlife trade are the driving forces behind the increasing number of diseases leaping from wildlife to humans.[24] All of our recent pandemics have had their origin in the human interaction between humans and wild animals, stressed by the destruction of their habitat and the brutal treatment they have received from humans. Artemis warns us that if our species is to survive we must abandon the fantasy that our health and our relationship to nature are not intimately connected.

As goddess of childbirth Artemis has a special role in the protection of children. She is the centre of an alternative world which does not accept male domination and exploitation and the taken-for-grantedness of patriarchal values. She provides an alternative to the 'new normal' being planned by our leaders.

We need to include Hestia, the maiden aunt in the Olympian family, who inspires us to ignore the noise and frenzy and quietly get on with our weaving. Hestia is the centre of things. She is the centre of the individual, the centre of the family, the centre of the city, the centre of the world. She is most certainly the god of sitting quietly at home. She represents the place of stillness from which we come and to which we go, the point around which everything revolves. We can see in our current situation how she gives us a new focus on our family and how she drives people in service professions to engage selflessly and without any fuss in the service of others. We can see also how she is now providing a context in which people can express or rediscover their creativity. It is the voice of Hestia which currently ends our emails or phone conversations with 'Stay safe'.

We also need to worship Hephaistos, Aphrodite's husband. He is the divine blacksmith, the god of craftwork. Indeed, he is the only god who works. Hephaistos is the ugly god, who creates beauty through pain and tedium. His status rose enormously during the golden age of Athens, along with the status of his worshippers, and fell again as the metal-workers, potters, sculptors, wood- workers and jewellers fell in the social hierarchy. We feel a new appreciation for the dedication and skills of the workers, often poorly paid, who are now keeping society alive by teaching, nursing, driving trucks and stacking shelves.

We hope that this respect will last longer than the plague. Work has a major place in the current rhetoric but unfortunately it is the market value of work which is alleged to give it meaning, not the discomfort human beings in our culture feel when they deny their yearning to create something beautiful and meaningful through work, or when they are frustrated in their attempts to do so.

In the Academy in Athens, there was a shrine dedicated to Prometheus, as divine patron of the Arts and Sciences. Prometheus was not one of the Olympians, but he was greatly honoured, revered as the saviour of humanity, the god who actually took the side of humanity against the will and wrath of Zeus. The image of Prometheus has been enormously significant in European consciousness. He is the benefactor who brought the gift of technology down from heaven, the teacher who showed us that we are not at the whim of the gods anymore, who taught us how to use our intelligence to take control of the world. We feel the energy of Prometheus in our confidence that we will get control of this invisible enemy and that it is our intelligent use of technology which will make this possible.

We should be aware also of the power of Nemesis, the goddess of justice and vengeance, the Greek equivalent of Karma. The gods, as the Greeks understood them, do not care too much about human morality. The only sin which bothers them is hubris, human beings' delusional conviction that they are somehow significant and powerful, and that they do not need to show respect for the gods. It is Nemesis' task to punish people who think too highly of themselves. We find Nemesis within us when we feel the urge to 'get even', when we feel that justice has been served, when we experience schadenfreude at seeing someone 'get what's coming to them', including Trump supporters who, with his support, ignore the medical advice on physical and social distancing. We can see Nemesis at work in the conviction within some religious sects that COVID19 is the Christian God's punishment for our neglect of His laws, or in the parallel conviction among Gaia worshippers that the approaching climate catastrophe is Gaia's revenge for the way we have treated Her.

The myth of Persephone, the goddess of Spring, represents the same death-rebirth theme as the identification of Dionysus with Hades. She is both Hades' consort, the Queen of Death, and the girl-goddess who returns to earth every springtime. She reminds us that rebirth demands a death. In the Persephone myth, it is Hermes who negotiates with Hades for her annual return to the light. We should understand that we will not have a new world unless we are prepared, Hermes-like, to let the 'normal' one die.

According to myth, Poseidon is the elder brother of Zeus, who fought at his side in the war against the Titans and who, in the settlement which followed, took the sea as his domain while Zeus took the sky and their other brother, Hades, took charge of the Underworld. Poseidon, like Zeus, is the personification of power, but he is a rather rougher character than his younger brother. Poseidon-power is deep, unknowable, sometimes calm and friendly but often unpredictably violent. It is expressed in catastrophic events, like earthquakes and storms at sea. Mere mortals cannot resist it; their only hope is to ride out its turbulence. In the current catastrophe, we can see Poseidon at work in the suggestion that we should stop trying to solve this unsolvable problem through technology and social distancing and let the plague do its stuff. Inevitably many will die, but we lucky few will survive through gaining 'tribal immunity'. We do not have to take this extreme view to acknowledge that sometimes bad things happen and we may not always be able to do anything about it. The notion that we can always be in control is delusional.

Zeus and his family, who dwelled on Mount Olympus, were not the only gods demanding worship. Pan and Priapus, Hekate and Hypnos, the Graces, the Muses, the Fates and the Furies, were all alive in the Greek awareness of the world, and they are still competing for our attention when we turn our minds to confronting the present crisis.

Jungian theory supports the Greeks' conviction that unacknowledged gods are dangerous. If we do not give a particular aspect of our personality a place in our awareness, it will take over our behaviour from time to time to our distress or embarrassment. We will do or say something which comes from a part of us with which we do not identify, and we will attempt to justify it with 'I was not myself', or 'Something came over me.' It is only when we acknowledge our capacity for violence, bitchiness or prejudice that we are able to control it.

The same can be said of the archetypes at the cultural level. If collectively we ignore our need to share power, we get revolution. If we ignore our need for power we end up with dictatorship. If we ignore the groundlessness of the global financial system we are shocked by the GFC. If we do not satisfy our need for beauty we are flooded with pornography.

Summoned or not

Each of the gods has his or her special gifts to give. Each represents a different notion of the purpose of life, a different perspective on reality, a different energy driving our behaviour. Each god has a truth, an ethics and an aesthetics which must be respected, even though they may contradict each other.

Zeus tells us to respect rightful authority; Apollo tells us to act rationally; Hera tells us to fulfil our social obligations; Aphrodite tell us to pursue beauty; Artemis demands that we must live in harmony with Nature; Hephaistos tells us that work is honourable; Eros helps us to love one another; Poseidon reminds us that bad things happen; Dionysus challenges us to become fully ourselves; Hermes tells us to be flexible and adaptable and worship all the gods; Athena tells us to keep things in balance; Prometheus requires us to use our intelligence to make a better world; Ares wants us approach our tasks with passion; Hestia gently suggests that we stay centred and focus on what is essential.

Jung's theory of archetypes is essentialist. He is telling us that this is the way the world is. However, from a structuralist perspective, this is only part of the story. The Greek gods may individually represent deep structures, but together they are manifestations of a deeper structure - the Greek pantheon. This is not the foundation structure for perceptions of our psychological and social being, but simply one pantheon among many - Celtic, Nordic, Asian, African, Australian, Pacific, American - as well as others which are outside the reach of our imagination. What is important for us here is that the particular set of energies which shaped the consciousness of the ancient Greeks are the energies of a patriarchal culture struggling with the notions of human freedom and political participation and simultaneously intent on following Apollo's injunction to keep women subservient.[25] Very like our own.

We may like to see the eternally squabbling gods simply as colourful images, and their worship simply a useful metaphor to help us explore a multi-dimensional approach to reality. On the other hand, we may wish to take them more seriously, to acknowledge that the Greeks, like other polytheistic cultures, knew something about cosmology and psychology which we have forgotten. We may as readily approach ultimate reality through a fantasy of the Many as through a fantasy of the One.[26] Whatever our religious beliefs, it can be argued that psychologically we are polytheistic. Whether we summon them or not, the gods are present.[27]

References

[1] See B.Neville The Charm of Hermes: Hillman, Lyotard and the Postmodern Condition. *Journal of Analytical Psychology*, July 1992, 337-353.

[2] Joseph Campbell, *The Masks of God.* Viking, 1968.

[3] Collected Works 7. Princeton University Press, 1966, p.109.

[4] The cultural philosopher Jean Gebser argued that alongside the rational structure of consciousness with which we tend to identify we have a mythical structure of conscious. We think we are making rational decisions when we are simply caught up in a culturally embedded myth whose truth we take for granted. See Jean Gebser. *The Ever Present Origin.* Ohio University Press 1986 (1951).

[5] See S. Pinker *How the Mind Works*, Penguin, 1997. Pinker suggests that our genes carry even such abstract notions as a sense of justice and a sense of self.

[6] For discussion of image schemas see M. Johnson, *The Body in the Mind: the bodily basis of meaning, imagination and reason.* University of Chicago Press, 1987; G. Lakoff, *Women, Fire and Dangerous Things; what categories reveal about the mind.* University of Chicago Press, 1987.

[7] The philosopher Alfred North Whitehead speaks of the universe as being composed of 'drops of experience', an expression he borrowed from William James.

[8] Epiminides (c.500 B.C.) quoted by St Paul in Acts, xvii, 28. The idea which the Greek philosophers developed of Zeus as a supreme and benevolent deity owed a great deal to the increasing influence of Judaism.

[9] Arthur Schopenhauer. *The World as Will and Idea*. CreateSpace Independent Publishing Platform (1818) 2018

[10] James Lovelock. *The Revenge of Gaia*. Penguin, 2006.

[11] Donna Haraway argues that labelling our epoch 'anthropocene' is misleading. It should more appropriately be called the 'chthulucene' era to indicate the human and nonhuman are inextricably linked.

We are part of the damaged earth, not observers or controllers of it. See D. Haraway, *Staying with the Trouble: Making Kin in the Chthulucene*. Duke University Press, 2016.

[12] The Cretans (Minoans) had cultural (and occasionally political) dominance of southern Greece between 2000 and 1400 B.C. The bronze-age Mycenean culture which is described by Homer in the Iliad and Odyssey, was the product of an enthusiastic acceptance of the Cretan civilisation by the invading Minyans.

[13] The Dorians were a Indo-European people who seem to have entered the peninsula c. 1200 B.C. and settled in central and southern Greece.

[14] Jurgen Habermas. *The Theory of Communicative Action*. Polity, 1986.

[15] In *Solitude* Anthony Storr argues that our capacity for being alone is just as important an aspect of psychological health as our capacity for relationship. See *Solitude*. Harper Collins, 1997.

[16] Alfred North Whitehead. *Science and Method*. Dover, 2003 [1914]), p.22.

[17] John Keats, Ode to a Grecian Urn.

[18] Alfred North Whitehead, *Adventures in Ideas*, Cambridge University Press, 1933, p,272.

[19] Whitehead, *Modes of Thought*, Touchstone Books, 1968. pp. 158-59.

[20] Hesiod. *Theogony.* Trans. A.Athanassakis, Johns Hopkins University Press, 2004, p. 83.

[21] Compare the Nordic Loki, the Irish Lugh and the Roman Mercury.

[22] A. Athanassakis. *The Homeric Hymns.* Johns Hopkins University Press. 2004.

[23] See James Hillman. *Archetypal Psychology: a brief account.* Spring Publications, 1983.

[24] The Guardian, 27 March 2020.

[25] Apollo's temple at Delphi had this instruction carved in its lintel.

[26] See David Miller. *The New Polytheism.* Spring publications, 1981.

[27] Above the door of his home Jung carved the words: 'Vocatus aut non vocatus deus aderit.'